Toe Ticklers

Foot-Shaped Bible Crafts

Lori Miescke

Illustrated By Steve Edwards

CPH
SAINT LOUIS

To my daughter
Juliane for her help and
suggestions for this book

Copyright © 1999 Concordia Publishing House
3558 S. Jefferson Avenue, St. Louis, MO 63118-3968

Manufactured in the United States of America

1 2 3 4 5 6 7 8 9 10   08 07 06 05 04 03 02 01 00 99

Footnotes

These 30 craft ideas will make Bible study inspirational and fun while teaching and motivating children. Each toe-tickling project begins with a foot-shaped pattern and ends with Bible-based teaching suggestions.

The easy-to-complete crafts require a minimum of adult help. Every craft has a Scripture verse, list of required materials, step-by-step directions, and suggestions for use. All patterns are reproducible. When patterns are included on the list of necessary materials, make one photcopy on white paper per child. The materials are listed as needed for each child. The number of children completing the project will determine the amount of materials needed.

It is my hope that children will enjoy completing these foot-shaped, toe-tickling crafts as they learn about God's love. So get set for some toe-tickling fun!

The Author

Contents

Abraham Puppet

"I will surely bless you and make your descendants as numerous as the stars in the sky and as the sand on the seashore."
Genesis 22:17

To Get

Lightweight poster board
Scissors
Markers
Glue
Craft sticks or rulers

To Do

1. Trace two footprints on lightweight poster board.
2. Color gown and head. Cut out.
3. Glue both pieces together. Leave bottom of footprints open.
4. Place ruler or craft stick inside footprints.
5. Add gown and head.

To Follow Up

- Use the Abraham puppet to tell how God tested Abraham (Genesis 22:1–19).

- Have the children use the puppet to retell the story to each other.

Glue heel here

Glue footprints, except toes

Angel

 How beautiful are the feet of those who bring Good News! Romans 10:15

To Get

Lightweight poster board

White construction paper

Scissors

Markers

Paintbrush

Glue

Water

Hole punch

String

Silver glitter

Gold cord

To Do

1. Trace two footprints on lightweight poster board for each child.
2. Color and cut out.
3. Glue one footprint to other along heel sections to make wings.
4. Dilute glue with water. Paint wings with watered-down glue. Shake silver glitter over wings.
5. Trace gown and head on white construction paper.
6. Cut out and glue head on gown. Glue angel figure to center of wings.
7. Glue gold cord around top of head for halo.
8. Punch a hole in top of angel. Attach string as hanger.

Glue head here

Glue footprints for wings

Glue arms here

To Follow Up

- Display the angels from doorways, windows, or on Christmas trees as holiday decorations.

- Encourage the children to hang their angels in their bedrooms as a reminder of God's protection.

Bee

 All men are like grass, and all their glory is like the flowers of the field; the grass withers and the flowers fall, but the Word of the Lord stands forever.
1 Peter 1:24–25

To Get

Yellow construction paper

Black construction paper

Black pipe cleaners

Scissors

Glue

Crayons

Hole punch

String

To Do

1. Trace footprint, head, and wings on black construction paper.
2. Cut out.
3. Glue head and wings on footprint to make bee.
4. Cut strips from yellow paper and glue on bee's body. Leave some black showing.
5. Supply each child with one 4-inch length of pipe cleaner. Glue these to head for antennae.
6. Use crayons to color eyes and mouth.
7. Punch a hole in top of bee. Add string as hanger.

Cut one wing in reverse

Bend pipe cleaner
and tape or glue to
back of head

To Follow Up

- Display the bees in a
  window as a reminder
  of God's handiwork.

- Display on a Bulletin
  Board that urges
  children to "Bee in
  the Word."

Boat

Then He got up and rebuked the winds and the waves, and it was completely calm.
Matthew 8:26

To Get

Lightweight poster board
Blue construction paper
Black construction paper
White construction paper
Scissors
Glue
Crayons

To Do

1. Provide each child with a sheet of black construction paper.
2. Trace pattern A on lightweight poster board. Color and cut out.
3. Trace four of pattern B on blue construction paper. Cut out.
4. Trace pattern C on white paper. Cut out and glue to sheet of black construction paper.
5. Glue pattern A on sheet of black construction paper, leaving top edge of foot open like a boat.
6. Trace people on white paper. Cut out and slip into top edge of boat.
7. Glue waves (pattern B) around boat.

Pattern B   Pattern A   Pattern C

Patterns for the Boat

To Follow Up

● Use the boat to tell the story of how Jesus calmed the storm (Matthew 8:23–27).

● Have the children use their boats to roleplay the Bible story.

Top open

Glue

Bookmark

He will teach us His ways, so that we may walk in His paths. Isaiah 2:3

To Get

Blue construction paper
Scissors
Glue
8-inch pieces of colored ribbon
Glitter

To Do

1. Trace footprint on blue construction paper. Cut out.
2. Supply children with three 8-inch pieces of colored ribbon.
3. Show children how to glue ribbon to back of footprint as shown in diagram.
4. Add glue around outer edge of footprint. Sprinkle with glitter.

To Follow Up

- Ask the children to give the bookmark to Mom or Dad so they have a bookmark that displays a verse from God's Word.

- The children can use them as a bookmark for their own Bibles.

He will
teach us
His ways,
so that we
may walk in
His paths.

Isaiah 2:3

Boy Puppet

 We live by faith, not by sight.
2 Corinthians 5:7

To Get

Lightweight poster board
Pieces of brightly colored felt
Scissors
Glue
Markers
Rulers or craft sticks

To Do

1. Trace footprint, hands, and head on lightweight poster board.
2. Color and cut out.
3. Supply each child with robe pattern drawn on felt. Cut out.
4. Glue felt robe on footprint, leaving bottom of robe unglued.
5. Glue head and hands on robe.
6. Glue ruler or craft stick inside footprint. Draw a foot on the exposed toe as shown in diagram.

To Follow Up

- Use the boy puppet to tell the Bible story of 12-year-old Jesus as He visited the temple in Jerusalem (Luke 2:41–51).

- Have the children use the puppet to retell the Bible story.

Cut gown from felt

Butterfly

The skies proclaim the work of His hands.
Psalm 19:1B

To Get

Lightweight poster board

Scissors

Glue

Water

Paintbrush

Colored glitter

Markers

Black pipe cleaners

Hole punch

String

To Do

1. Trace two footprints and one body pattern on lightweight poster board.
2. Color and cut out.
3. Glue footprints together as shown in diagram.
4. Glue body on wings and bend footprints upward.
5. Supply each child with one 4-inch length of black pipe cleaner.
6. Curl each end of pipe cleaner and glue to head of butterfly.
7. Dilute glue with water. Paint wings of butterfly with watered-down glue. Shake glitter over wings.

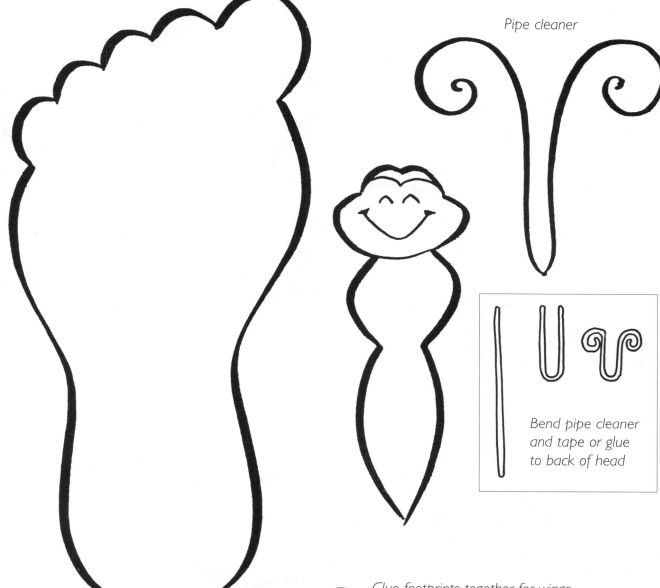

Pipe cleaner

Bend pipe cleaner and tape or glue to back of head

Glue footprints together for wings

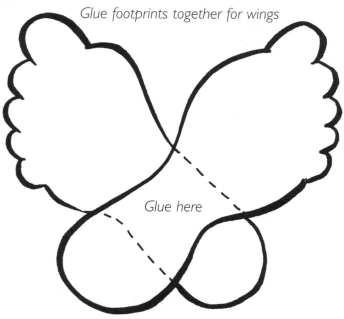

Glue here

To Follow Up

- Punch a hole in the butterfly. Hang with a string to display for all to see.

- Complete this project at Easter to remind the children of the new life that is theirs because of Christ's death and resurrection.

Camel

"Again I tell you, it is easier for a camel to go through the eye of a needle than for a rich man to enter the kingdom of God." Matthew 19:24

To Get

Brown construction paper

Paper plate

Scissors

Glue

Water

Paintbrush

Crayons

Sand

To Do

1. Trace one large and two small footprints on brown construction paper. Trace the head and tail on brown construction paper.
2. Color and cut out.
3. Glue head and tail to large footprint as shown. Bend head upwards as shown in diagram.
4. Fold smaller footprints on dotted line and glue to back of larger footprints to form camel's humps.
5. Dilute glue with water. Paint bottom of paper plate with watered-down glue. Shake sand over glue.
6. Place folded part of small footprints on paper plate so camel appears to be resting.

Glue to toes

hump

fold line

bend backward

To Follow Up

- Display the completed camels for all to see.

- Use the camels to tell Bible stories such as the journey to Bethlehem (Luke 2:1–7) or Palm Sunday (Matthew 21:1–9).

Glue   Glue

Candle

You, O LORD, keep my lamp burning; my God turns my darkness into light. Psalm 18:28

To Get

Lightweight poster board
Orange construction paper
Gold cord
Scissors
Paintbrush
Glue
Water
Brightly colored markers
Gold glitter

To Do

1. Trace footprint and candle pattern on lightweight poster board. Cut out.
2. Trace flame pattern on orange construction paper. Cut out.
3. Glue footprint to candle as shown. Glue flame inside candle and fold as shown in diagram.
4. Dilute glue with water and paint watered-down glue on flame. Sprinkle with gold glitter.
5. Instruct the children to use brightly colored markers to decorate the candle holder.
6. Outline edges of footprint with glue and add gold cord.
7. Write Bible verse on candle.

fold line

Glue

Glue

Fold

To Follow Up

- Place candles near the entrance of the sanctuary to help spread the Word of God.

- Urge the children to display their candles at home to remind them that God's Word lights the way.

Dove

Then [Noah] sent out a dove to see if the water had receded from the surface of the Ground. Genesis 8:8

To Get

Lightweight poster board
Green construction paper
A thin twig
Scissors
Markers
Glue
Black marker
Hole punch
String

To Do

1. Trace two footprints and pattern A on lightweight poster board and cut out.
2. Flip one footprint so there is a left footprint and a right footprint. Color each footprint.
3. Fold each footprint on dotted line. Glue heel of each footprint to corresponding side of dove to form wings.
4. Trace pattern B on green construction paper. Cut out.
5. Glue leaves to end of twig.
6. Glue twig in dove's beak.

To Follow Up

- Punch a hole in the top of each dove and add a string as a hanger. Display in a window.

- Use the dove to tell the story of Noah's ark (Genesis 8:6–12).

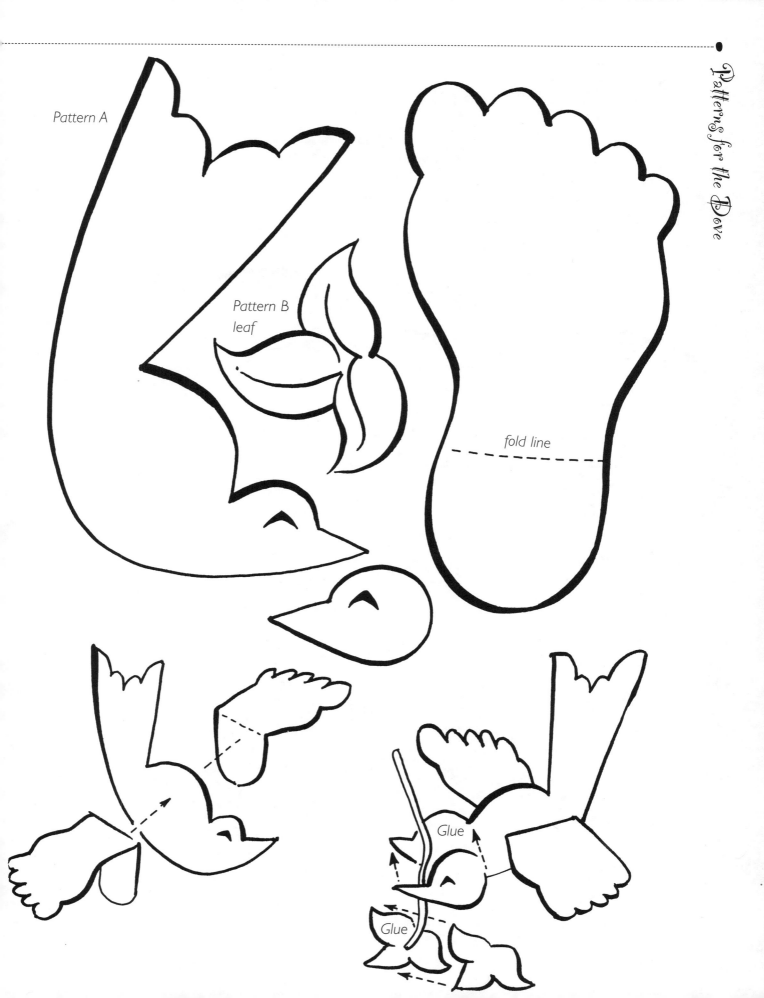

Pattern A

Pattern B
leaf

fold line

Glue

Glue

Footprint Ruler

"Give, and it will be given to you. A good
measure, pressed down, shaken together
and running over, will be poured into
your lap. For with the measure you use,
it will be measured to you." Luke 6:38

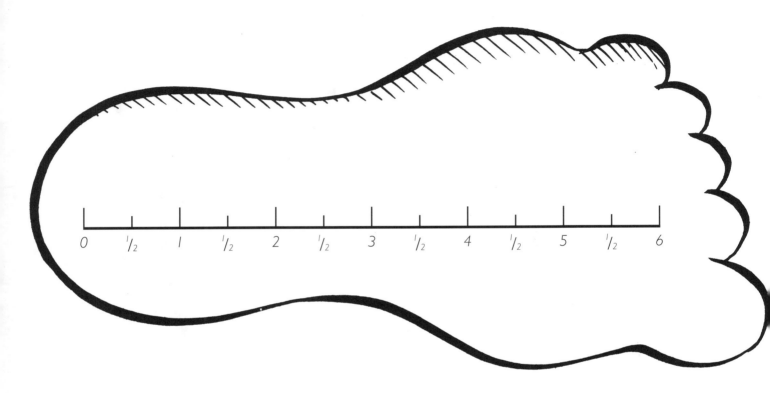

To Get

Lightweight poster board

Scissors

Black marker

Markers

Ruler

To Do

1. Trace footprint on lightweight poster board.
2. Color and cut out.
3. Use black marker and ruler to mark footprint into ½-inch and 1-inch measurements as shown in diagram.
4. Use markers of assorted colors to decorate footprint ruler.

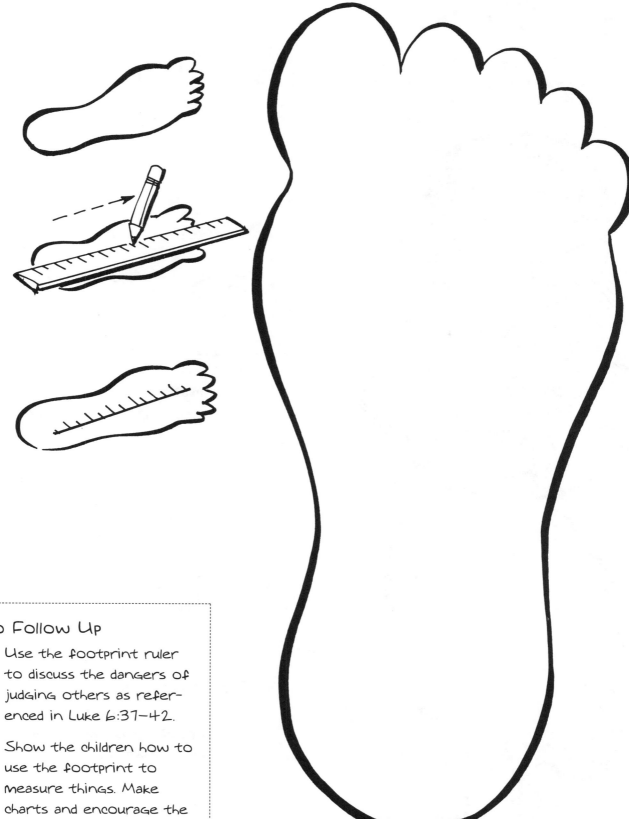

To Follow Up

• Use the footprint ruler
  to discuss the dangers of
  judging others as referenced in Luke 6:37–42.

• Show the children how to
  use the footprint to
  measure things. Make
  charts and encourage the
  children to measure items
  in their environment.

Girl Puppet

"I tell you the truth, anyone who will not receive the kingdom of God like a little child will never enter it." Luke 18:17

To Get

Lightweight poster board
Pieces of brightly colored felt
Scissors
Glue
Markers
Rulers or craft sticks

To Do

1. Trace footprint, hands, and head on lightweight poster board.
2. Color and cut out.
3. Supply each child with robe pattern drawn on felt. Cut out.
4. Glue felt robe on footprint. Leave bottom of robe open.
5. Glue head and hands on robe.
6. Place ruler or craft stick inside footprint.

To Follow Up

● Use the Girl puppet to tell the story of Jesus Blessing the children (Matthew 19:13–14).

● Use the Girl puppet to tell the story of Jesus raising Jairus' daughter (Luke 8:40–42, 49–56).

Head

Shoulders

Glue foot here

Cut gown from felt

Joseph Puppet

[Jacob] made a richly ornamented robe for [Joseph]. Genesis 37:3

To Get

Lightweight poster board
Scissors
Glue
Brightly colored markers
Rulers or craft sticks

To Do

1. Trace all patterns on lightweight poster board.
2. Color with bright markers and cut out.
3. Glue head to shoulders. Glue shoulders to footprint.
4. Glue gown to footprint. Leave toe open.
5. Place ruler or craft stick inside puppet.

To Follow Up

- Use the Joseph puppet to tell the story of Joseph and his coat of many colors (Genesis 37).

- Have each child hold the Joseph puppet and practice using words of forgiveness, modeling the way Joseph forgave his brothers (Genesis 50:15–21).

Glue
to
shoulders

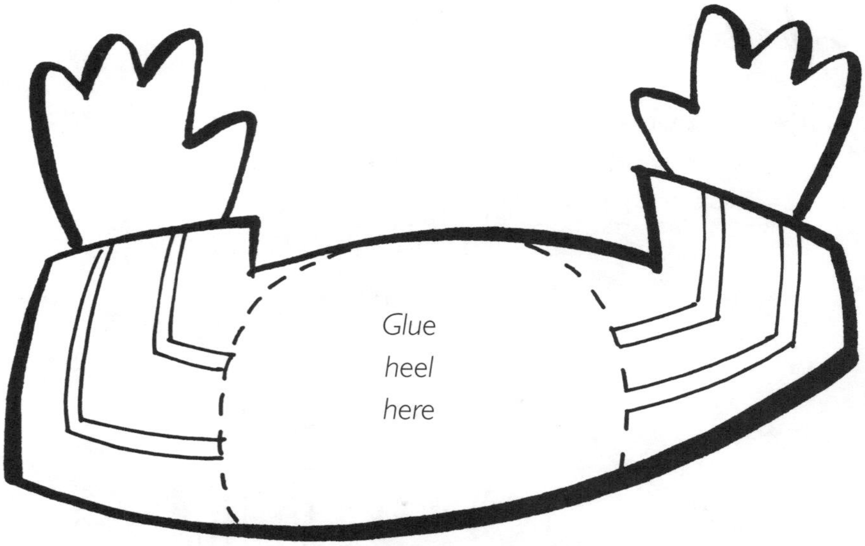

Glue
heel
here

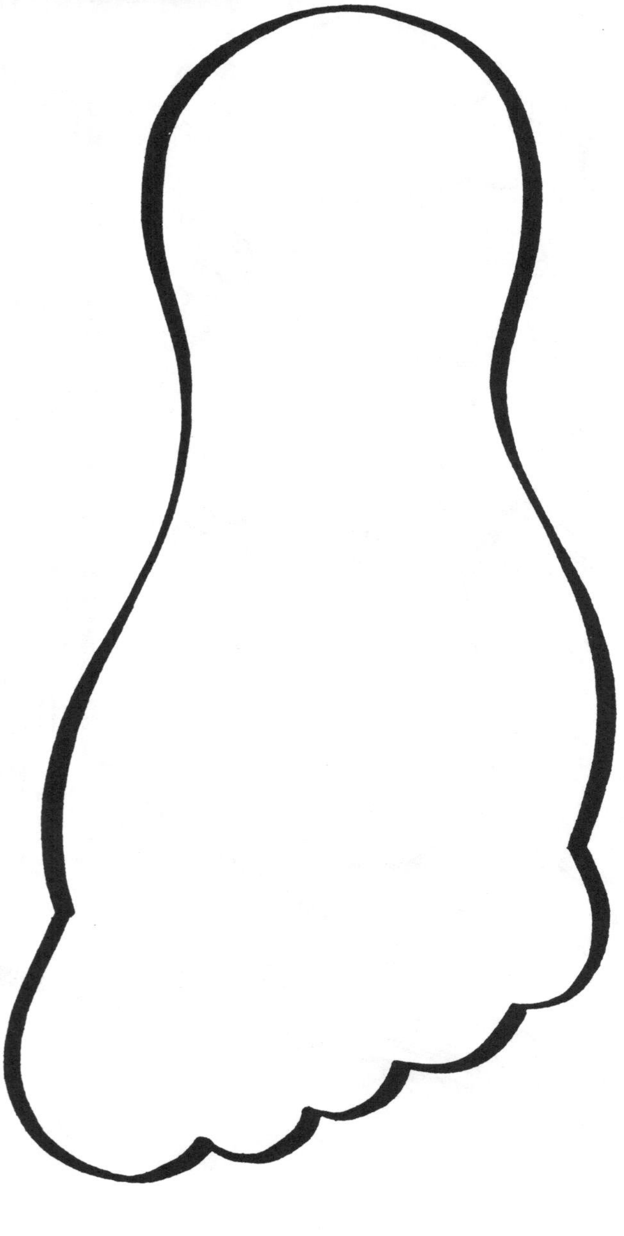

Journal

When you walk, your steps will not be hampered; when you run, you will not stumble. Proverbs 4:12

To Get

Two 9-inch × 12-inch sheets of red construction paper

White construction paper

Three-hole notebook paper, 12 sheets per child

Glue

Markers

Scissors

Hole punch

Paper fasteners

To Do

1. Place 12 sheets of three-hole paper between two sheets of red construction paper.
2. Punch holes in red construction paper to match holes of paper inside. Use paper fasteners to secure pages together.
3. Trace or reproduce a footprint for each child on white construction paper.
4. Cut out and glue footprint to cover of journal.
5. Tell the children to use the pages to draw pictures of different things they do with their feet. Pictures also can be cut from magazines. Ideas to feature include walking, swimming, riding a bicycle, jumping, or skipping.

To Follow Up

- Write the Bible verse on the cover and display the journals.

- Send an extra journal home for the family to complete.

Pattern for the Journal

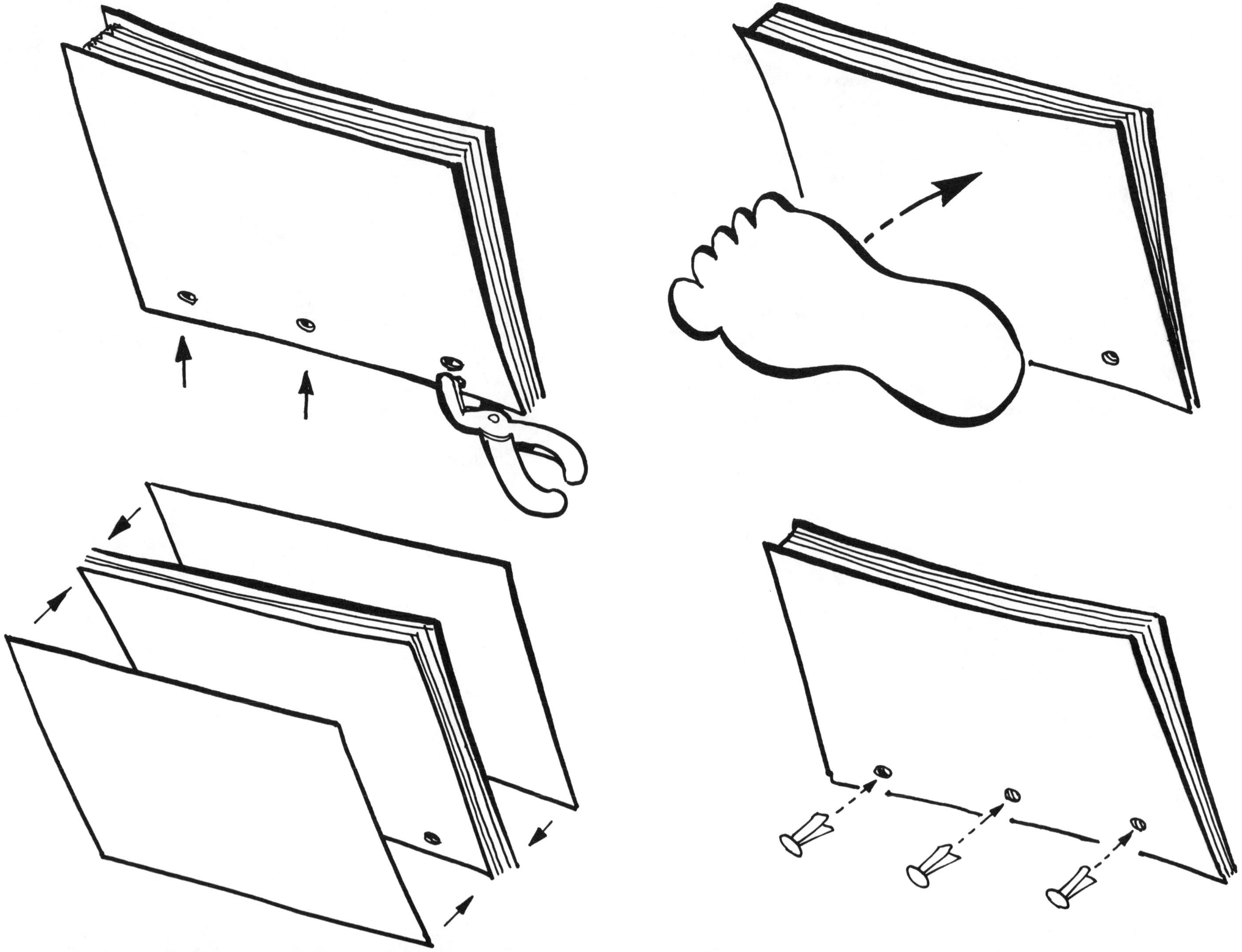

Key

"I will give you the keys of the kingdom of heaven." Matthew 16:19

"I will give you the keys of the kingdom of heaven." Matthew 16:19

To Get

Lightweight blue poster board
Aluminum foil
Scissors
Glue
Black marker
Crayons
Magnetic strip

To Do

1. Trace footprint on blue poster board. Cut out.
2. Provide each child with a pattern of key drawn on aluminum foil. Cut out.
3. Glue foil key on blue footprint.
4. Use black marker to write Bible verse on key.
5. Glue a strip of magnet to back side of footprint.

To Follow Up

- Use the footprint key to teach that the door to heaven is narrow (Luke 13:22–30).

- Use the footprint key to teach that believing in Jesus as the Savior who died for our sins and rose again is the key to entering heaven (John 11:25; John 14:6).

Glue magnet

King David Puppet

Show me Your ways, O LORD, teach me Your paths; guide me in Your truth and teach me, for You are God my Savior, and my hope is in You all day long. Psalm 25:4-5

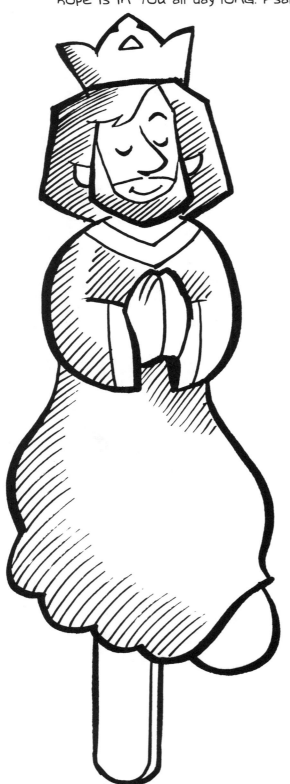

To Get

Lightweight poster board

Light blue construction paper

Gold glitter

Paintbrush

Scissors

Glue

Water

Markers

Rulers or craft sticks

To Do

1. Trace all patterns on lightweight poster board.
2. Color and cut out.
3. Glue gown piece on top of footprint. Leave bottom of footprint open.
4. Dilute glue with water. Paint crown with watered-down glue. Shake gold glitter over crown.
5. When crown is dry, fold tabs backward. Glue crown to head. Glue head and hands to footprint.
6. Place ruler or craft stick inside footprint.

To Follow Up

- Have children place the crown on the head of the puppet as you tell the story of Samuel anointing David king (1 Samuel 16:1–13).

- Use the King David puppet to teach about the book of Psalms.

Tab

Tab

Glue
to
heel

Kneeling Child

Then little children were brought to Jesus for Him to place His hands on them and pray for them. Matthew 19:13

To Get

Lightweight poster board
Scissors
Glue
Markers

To Do

1. Trace all patterns on lightweight poster board.
2. Color and cut out.
3. Glue heel of footprint to head. Glue arms to sides of body as shown in diagram.
4. Fold toes backward so child is kneeling.

To Follow Up

- Use the kneeling child to discuss ways to pray for others who walk to spread the Good News about Jesus.

- Paste the kneeling child on the front of a prayer journal, and use the journal for listing prayer requests.

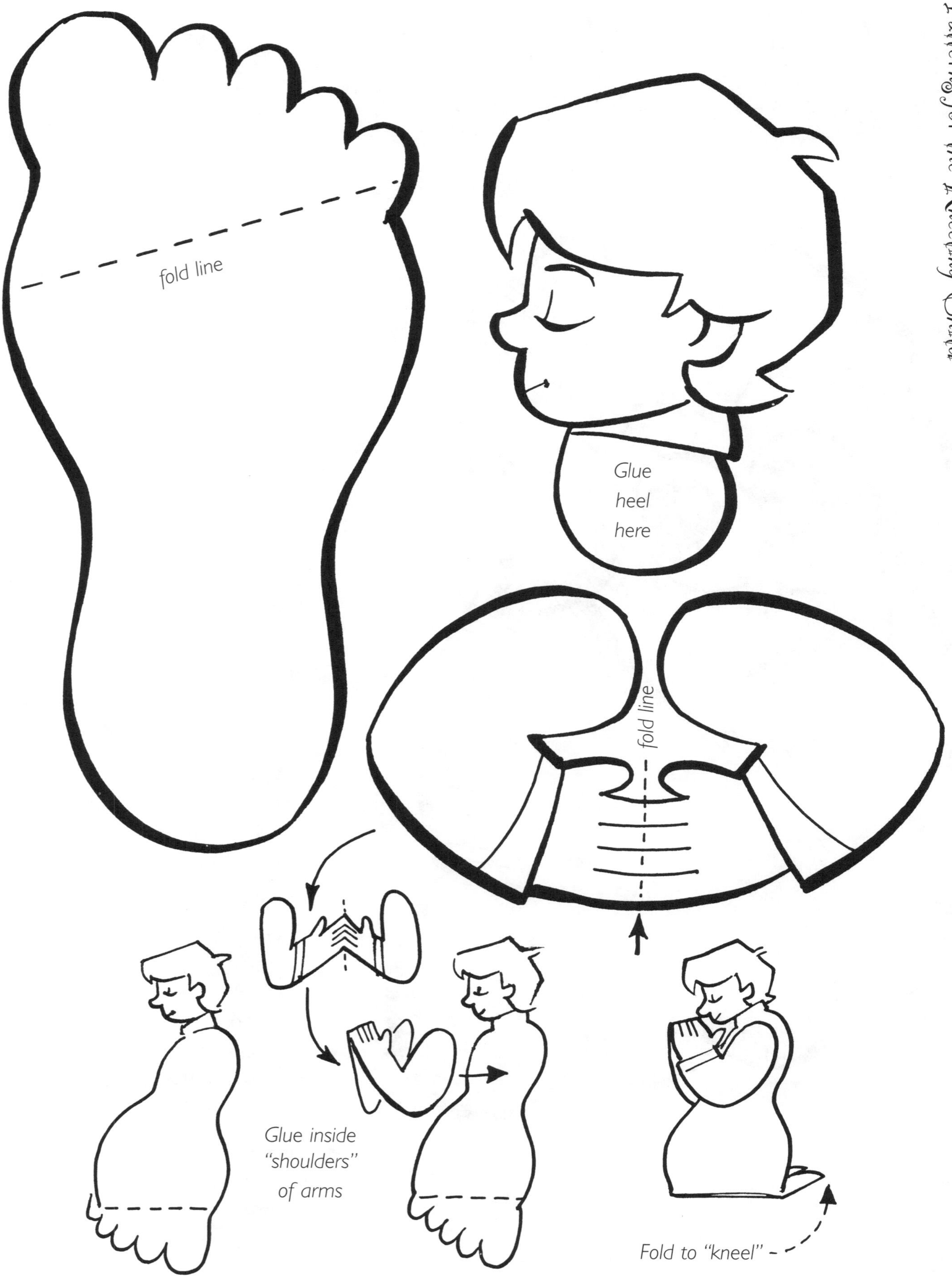

fold line

Glue
heel
here

fold line

Glue inside
"shoulders"
of arms

Fold to "kneel"

Lamb

The LORD is my shepherd, I shall not be in want.
Psalm 23:1

To Get

Black construction paper
White construction paper
Cotton balls
Scissors
Glue
Markers

To Do

1. Trace footprint and head pattern on black construction paper. Cut out.
2. Pull cotton balls apart and glue on toe portion of footprint.
3. Fold heel forward as shown in diagram.
4. Glue head to heel of footprint. Glue cotton to top of head.
5. Trace eyes and nose and cut out. Glue to heel portion of footprint.

To Follow Up

- Use the lamb to teach the parable of the lost sheep (Luke 15:1–7).

- Use the lamb to discuss ways that Jesus is the Good Shepherd (John 10:1–18).

Glue head here

fold line

Lily

Just as Christ was raised from the dead through the glory of the Father, we too may live a new life. Romans 6:4B

To Get

White construction paper
Green construction paper
Yellow pipe cleaners
Green pipe cleaners
Glue
Scissors
Green florist clay
Small flower pots or containers

To Do

1. Trace two footprints on white construction paper. Cut out.
2. Trace pattern for leaves on green construction paper. Cut out.
3. Glue one end of green pipe cleaner to one footprint. Follow diagram on pattern page to make leaves.
4. Glue the sides and bottom of second footprint to first footprint. Fold footprints on dotted lines as shown in diagram.
5. Follow diagram on pattern page to create stamens.
6. Press florist clay in bottom of flower pot or container. Secure bottom of green pipe cleaner into florist clay.

To Follow Up

- Display the pots of lilies on the windowsill and talk about the resurrection of Jesus (Luke 24:1–12).

- Discuss how God cares for all our needs as referenced in Matthew 6:25–34.

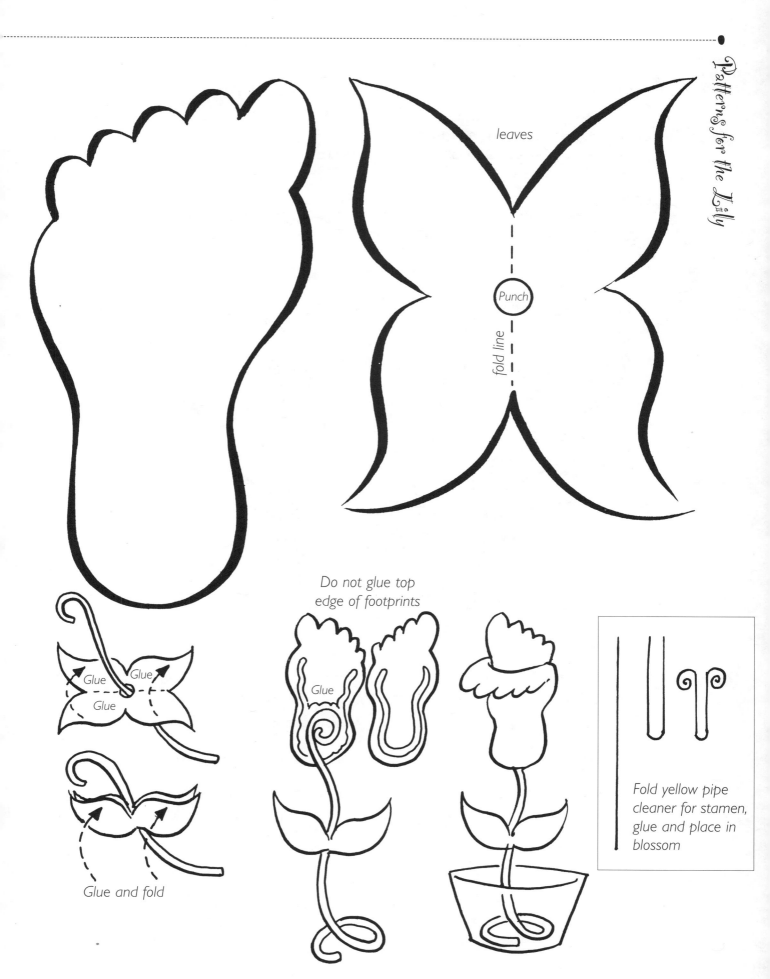

leaves

Punch

fold line

Do not glue top
edge of footprints

Glue   Glue

Glue

Glue

Glue and fold

Fold yellow pipe
cleaner for stamen,
glue and place in
blossom

Lion

The lions may grow weak and hungry, but those who seek the LORD lack no good thing. Psalm 34:10

42

To Get

Brown construction paper

Black pipe cleaners

Scissors

Markers

Glue

To Do

1. Trace two footprints on brown construction paper. Cut out.
2. Glue footprints together by overlapping heels as shown in diagram.
3. Color eyes and nose on face.
4. Trace and cut out two ears. Glue on footprints as shown in diagram.
5. Supply each child with two black pipe cleaners. Cut each pipe cleaner into three pieces.
6. Glue three pieces of pipe cleaner on each side of lion's face to represent whiskers.

Ear

*Overlap
footprints
and glue*

To Follow Up

- Use the lion to rein-
  force that God did not
  let the lions harm Daniel
  Because he trusted God
  and remained faithful
  (Daniel 6:1–23).

- Use the lion to discuss
  the peace and harmony
  of God's kingdom as
  referenced in Isaiah
  11:6–9.

Loaves and Fishes

Taking the five loaves and the two fish and looking up to heaven, [Jesus] gave thanks and broke the loaves. Mark 6:41

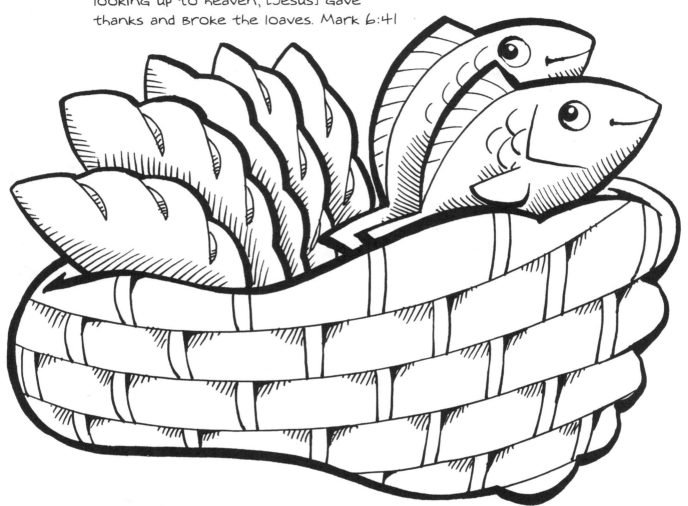

To Get

Yellow construction paper

White construction paper

Brown construction paper

Scissors

Glue

Crayons

To Do

1. Trace two footprints on yellow construction paper. Color and cut out.
2. Glue footprints together at sides and bottom to form basket.
3. Trace five loaf patterns on brown construction paper. Cut out.
4. Trace two fish patterns on white construction paper. Color and cut out.
5. Place five loaves and two fish in footprint basket.

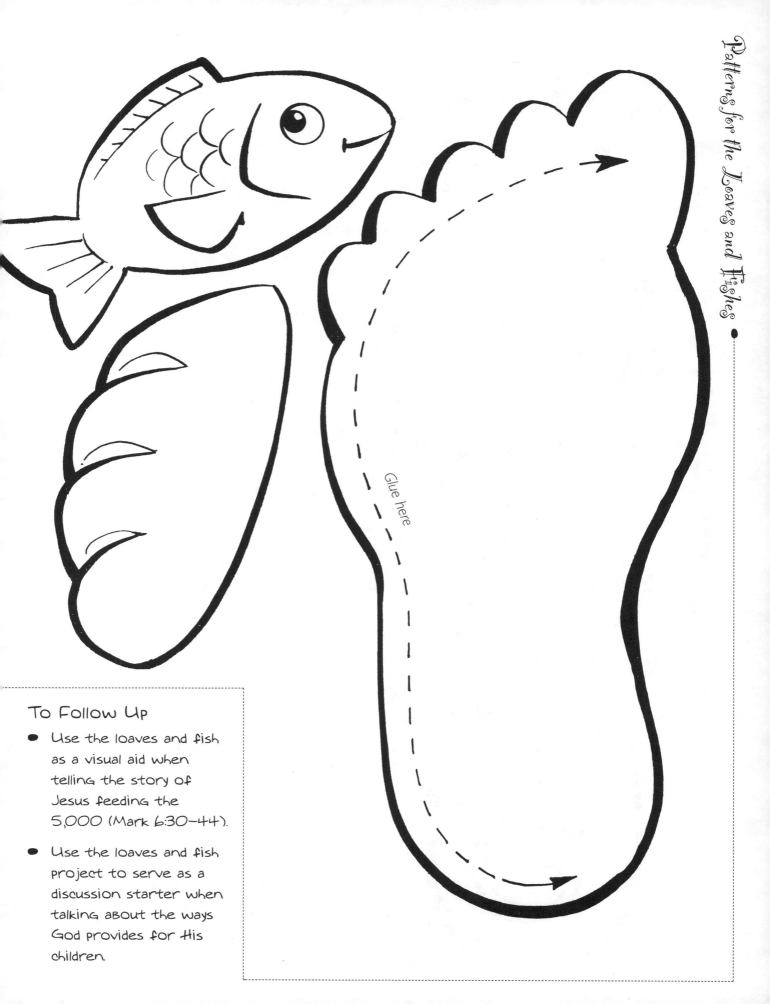

Glue here

To Follow Up

- Use the loaves and fish as a visual aid when telling the story of Jesus feeding the 5,000 (Mark 6:30–44).

- Use the loaves and fish project to serve as a discussion starter when talking about the ways God provides for His children.

Note Holder

He turned the sea into dry land, they passed through the waters on foot—come, let us rejoice in Him. Psalm 66:6

To Get

Lightweight poster board
Scissors
Glue
Markers
Magnetic strip
White paper, cut into 2-inch × 4-inch strips

To Do

1. Trace two footprints on lightweight poster board.
2. Color and cut out.
3. Glue footprints together. Leave toe portion open.
4. Use markers to decorate the front of the note holder.
5. Glue magnetic strip to back of note holder.
6. Supply each child with 2-inch × 4-inch pieces of white paper to fit inside note holder.

To Follow Up

- Use the note holder to tell how God opened the Red Sea so Moses could lead God's people across the sea on dry land (Exodus 14).

- Invite the children to write notes that share the love of Jesus with others.

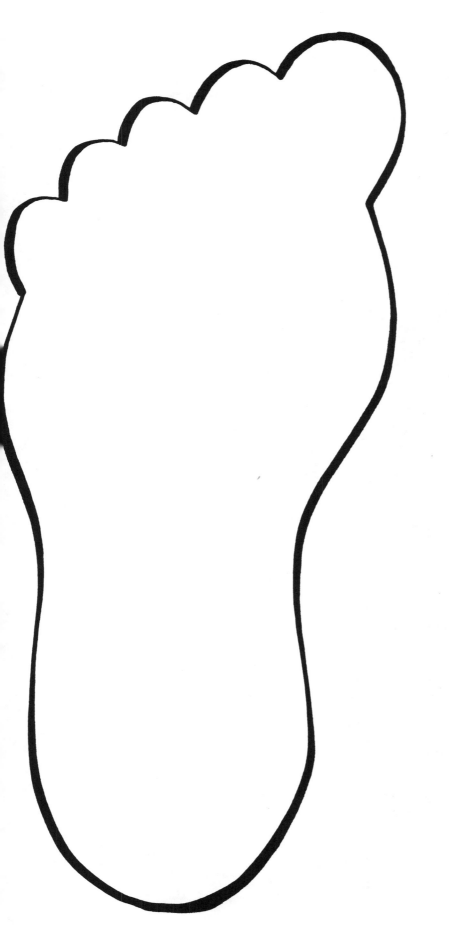

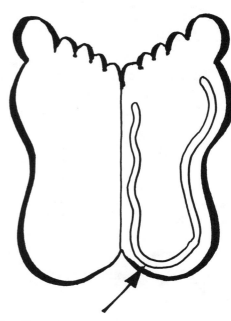

Glue footprints, except toes

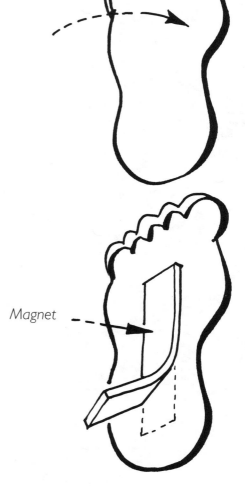

Magnet

Owl

 He who walks with the wise grows wise.
Proverbs 13:20a

To Get

Black construction paper
White construction paper
Gold paper
Scissors
Glue
Hole punch
String

To Do

1. Trace footprint on black construction paper. Cut out.
2. Trace two of Pattern A on white construction paper. Cut out.
3. Glue one Pattern A onto heel portion of footprint.
4. Trace two eyes, one beak, and two feet on gold paper.
5. Glue eyes, beak, and feet on face.
6. Cut other Pattern A apart as shown in diagram B to make wings and ears. Glue onto owl as shown in diagram.
7. Punch a hole in top of owl and attach a string.

To Follow Up

- Read the Bible verse to the children. Explain what it means to walk with the wise.

- Use the owl as a discussion starter to talk about the wisdom of God and His plan for our salvation (Romans 11:33–36).

Pattern A

Ear

B

Wing

Samuel Puppet

The LORD was with Samuel as he grew up.
1 Samuel 3:19

To Get

Lightweight poster board
Scissors
Markers
Glue
Rulers or craft sticks
Brown yarn

To Do

1. Trace all patterns on lightweight poster board.
2. Color and cut out.
3. Place head between heels of both footprints. Glue footprints together with head inside. *Do not glue bottom of footprints.*
4. Supply each child with brown yarn cut into 2-inch lengths.
5. Glue yarn on head to make Samuel's hair.
6. Place ruler or craft stick inside the bottom of the footprint.

To Follow Up

- Use the Samuel puppet to tell the Bible story of the Lord's call to young Samuel (1 Samuel 3:1–21).

- Encourage the children to use their puppets to roleplay the Bible story.

Glue between heels

Glue footprints,
except toes

Arm in front

Glue head and shoulders
between heels

Sandals

For You have delivered me from death and my feet from stumbling, that I may walk before God in the light of life. Psalm 56:13

Psalm 56:13

To Get

Lightweight poster board
Brown felt
Scissors
Glue
Markers
Yarn
Buttons

To Do

1. Trace one footprint and one strap on lightweight poster board. Cut out.
2. Trace one footprint and one strap on brown felt. Cut out.
3. Glue felt footprint to top side of poster board footprint.
4. Glue felt strap to one side of poster board strap.
5. Glue strap to bottom of footprint as shown in diagram.
6. Use markers to print "Psalm 56:13" on strap as shown in diagram. Decorate strap with buttons and yarn.

To Follow Up

- Use the sandals as a visual aid to tell the story of Joseph, Mary, and Jesus' escape to Egypt (Matthew 2:13–15).

- Use the sandals as a visual to tell how Jesus washed the feet of His disciples (John 13:1–17).

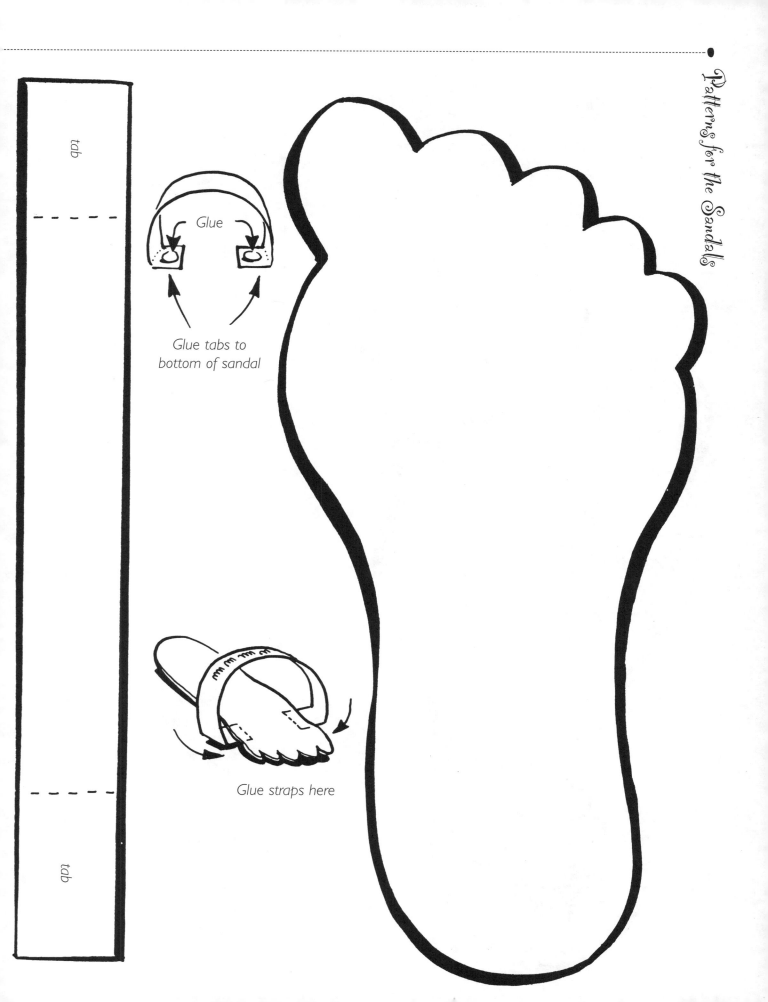

tab

Glue

Glue tabs to
bottom of sandal

Glue straps here

tab

Scripture Holder

And Jesus grew in wisdom and stature, and in favor with God and men. Luke 2:52

To Get

Blue construction paper
1½-inch × 3-inch strips of paper
Scissors
Glue
Markers
Bible

To Do

1. Trace two footprints on blue construction paper. Cut out.
2. Glue footprints together. Leave toe portion open.
3. Have the children label their footprint Scripture holder with their name and the words "Bible Verses" (see diagram).
4. Use markers to decorate Scripture holder.
5. Tell the children to print Bible verses they have learned on strips of paper, then place the verses in their Scripture holders.

To Follow Up

- Read and discuss the Bible verses with the children.

- Write out new Bible verses and add them as they are learned.

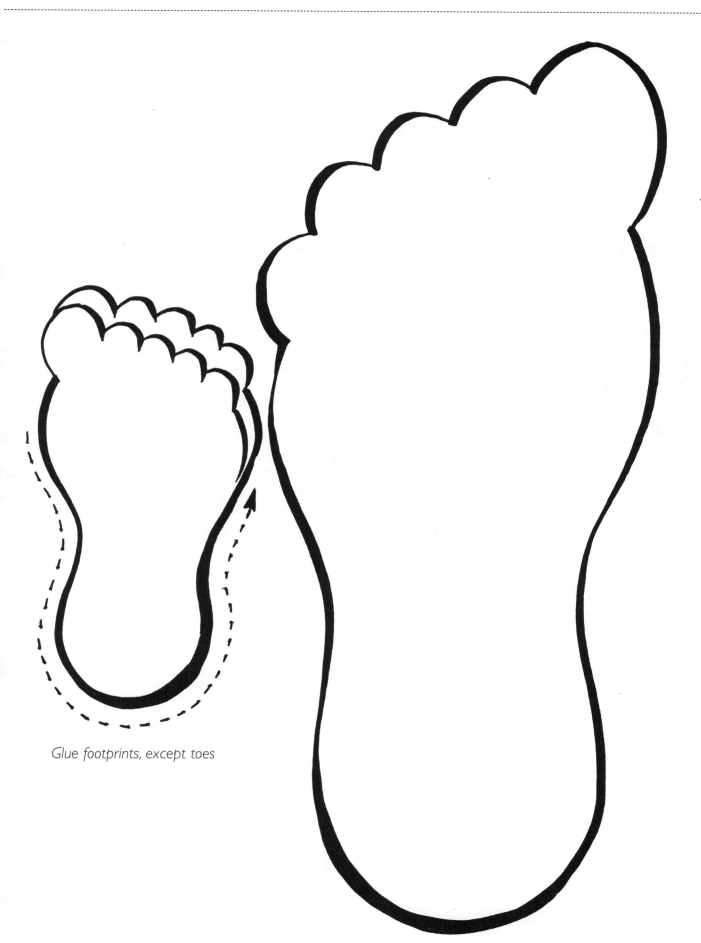

Glue footprints, except toes

Shepherd

"Today in the town of David a Savior has been born to you; He is Christ the Lord." Luke 2:11

To Get

White construction paper
Brown pipe cleaners, cut in half
Scissors
Glue
Crayons

To Do

1. Trace all patterns on white construction paper.
2. Color and cut out.
3. Supply each child with one pipe cleaner. Fold top to look like shepherd's staff.
4. Glue head and sleeve on footprint as shown in 4a and 4b.
5. Glue hands and pipe cleaner in place on shepherd as shown in 5a and 5b.

To Follow Up

- Tell how the shepherds hurried to find the Baby Jesus (Luke 2:8–16).

- Talk about ways to tell the Good News about Jesus, following the example of the shepherds (Luke 2:17).

Glue heel here

Glue heel here

4a

4b

5a

5b

Turtle

I have no greater joy than to hear that
my children are walking in the truth.
3 John:4

Walking
in the truth

To Get

Lightweight poster board
Blue construction paper
Scissors
Glue
Black marker
Markers

To Do

1. Trace one footprint, shell, head, and two small feet on lightweight poster board.
2. Color and cut out.
3. Glue shell, head, and small feet on footprint as indicated in diagram.
4. Trace one verse piece and five shell pieces on blue construction paper. Cut out.
5. Glue blue shell pieces and larger verse piece onto shell.
6. Use black marker to write "Walking in Truth" on verse piece.

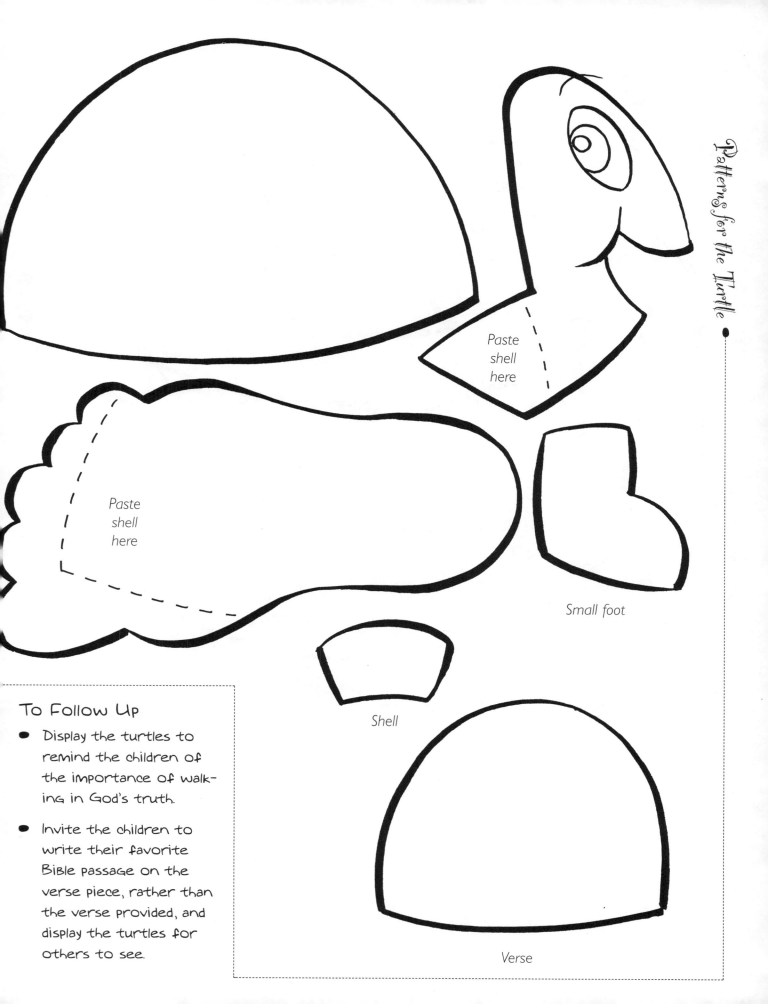

Pattern for the Turtle

Paste shell here

Paste shell here

Small foot

Shell

Verse

To Follow Up

- Display the turtles to remind the children of the importance of walking in God's truth.

- Invite the children to write their favorite Bible passage on the verse piece, rather than the verse provided, and display the turtles for others to see.

Vessel

Jesus answered her, "If you knew the Gift of God and who it is that asks you for a drink, you would have asked Him and He would have Given you living water." John 4:10

Jesus answered her, "If you knew the gift of God and who it is that asks you for a drink, you would have asked Him and He would have given you living water." John 4:10

To Get

Gold paper

8½-inch × 11-inch sheet of
   black construction paper

White construction paper

Blue tissue paper

Scissors

Glue

Black marker

To Do

1. Provide each child with black construction paper.
2. Trace vessel pattern on gold paper. Cut out.
   Cut along dotted line of vessel as indicated.
3. Glue sides and bottom of vessel to bottom half
   of black construction paper, leaving cut portion
   of vessel open.
4. Trace three footprints on white construction paper.
   Cut out footprints, and cover with blue tissue paper.
5. Place tissue-covered footprints inside vessel
   as shown in diagram.
6. Use black marker to write Bible verse on vessel.

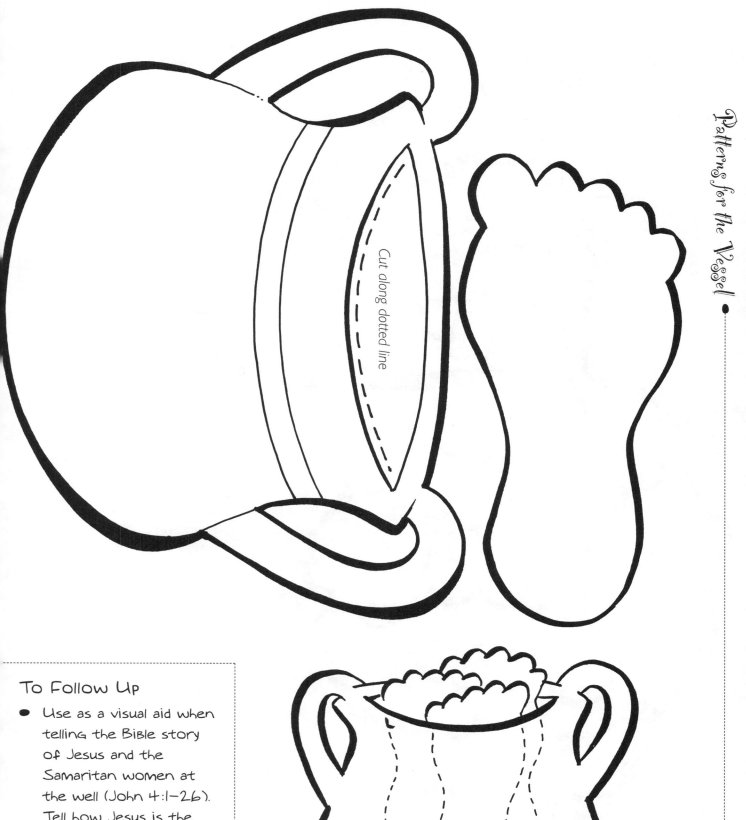

Cut along dotted line

To Follow Up

- Use as a visual aid when telling the Bible story of Jesus and the Samaritan women at the well (John 4:1–26). Tell how Jesus is the Living Water.

- Talk about why people had to get water from a well. Compare the way we live today with life in Bible times.

Zacchaeus' Tree

When Jesus reached the spot, He looked up and said to him, "Zacchaeus, come down immediately. I must stay at your house today." Luke 19:5

To Get

Tan construction paper
Green construction paper
White construction paper
Scissors
Glue
Markers

To Do

1. Trace tree trunk on tan construction paper. Cut out.
2. Supply each child with a sheet of green construction paper that has nine footprint patterns traced on it. Cut out footprints.
3. Glue tree trunk on sheet of white construction paper.
4. Fold footprints on dotted line and glue heels to the tree trunk to form leaves.
5. Trace Zacchaeus on white construction paper. Color and cut out. Glue Zacchaeus to top of tree, above leaves.

To Follow Up

- Place Zacchaeus in the tree as you tell the story of Zacchaeus the tax collector (Luke 19:1–9).

- Have the children sing the popular song "Zacchaeus Was a Wee Little Man" or use the tree to retell the Bible story.

fold line

Glue to top of tree, above leaves

Fold foot to make leaves